At Issue

| Sexting

Other Books in the At Issue Series

At Issue

| Sexting

Roman Espejo, Book Editor

GREENHAVEN PRESS
A part of Gale, Cengage Learning

GALE
CENGAGE Learning·

Farmington Hills, Mich • San Francisco • New York • Waterville, Maine
Meriden, Conn • Mason, Ohio • Chicago

Patricia Coryell, *Vice President & Publisher, New Products & GVRL*
Douglas Dentino, *Manager, New Products*
Judy Galens, *Acquisitions Editor*

For more information, contact:
Greenhaven Press
27500 Drake Rd.
Farmington Hills, MI 48331-3535
Or you can visit our Internet site at gale.cengage.com

For product information and technology assistance, contact us at

Gale Customer Support, 1-800-877-4253
For permission to use material from this text or product, submit all requests online at www.cengage.com/permissions.

Further permissions questions can be e-mailed to permissionrequest@cengage.com.

Articles in Greenhaven Press anthologies are often edited for length to meet page requirements. In addition, original titles of these works are changed to clearly present the main thesis and to explicitly indicate the author's opinion. Every effort is made to ensure that Greenhaven Press accurately reflects the original intent of the authors. Every effort has been made to trace the owners of copyrighted material.

Cover photograph copyright © Images.com/Corbis.

LIBRARY OF CONGRESS CATALOGING-IN-PUBLICATION DATA

Sexting / Roman Espejo, book editor.
    pages cm. -- (At issue)
  Includes bibliographical references and index.
  ISBN 978-0-7377-7185-5 (hardcover) -- ISBN 978-0-7377-7186-2 (pbk.)
  1. Sexting--Juvenile literature. 2. Teenagers--Sexual behavior. 3. Internet and teenagers--Juvenile literature. I. Espejo, Roman, 1977-
  HQ27.S4596 2015
  306.70285--dc23
                                                    2014030224

Printed in Mexico
1 2 3 4 5 6 7 19 18 17 16 15

Contents

Introduction

In 2011, "sexting" entered the *Concise Oxford English Dictionary*, defined as "the sending of sexually explicit photographs or messages via mobile phone." A combination of the words "sex" and "texting," it was coined in 2005 by the *Sunday Telegraph Magazine*, a publication in the United Kingdom. To prove that the term has become a part of everyday English language, sexting was submitted to a database of two billion words culled from the Internet and text messages. "It's how the dictionary has always worked—we get as much evidence as we can so we know it's not just a small number of people using the word and it's not going to disappear,"[1] states Angus Stevenson, head of dictionary projects at Oxford University Press.

A look at statistics from the Pew Research Internet Project indicates that sexting is not going away anytime soon. According to its 2013 survey of cell phone owners, 44 percent of eighteen- to twenty-four-year-olds have received "sexts" and 15 percent have sent sexts. In addition, 34 percent of twenty-five- to thirty-four-year-olds have received sexts and 22 percent have sent them. The figures decline significantly among older adults; 15 percent of forty-five- to fifty-four-year-olds have received sexts and 5 percent have sent sexts. As for adolescents, in 2010, the Pew Research Internet Project reported that 15 percent of twelve- to seventeen-year-olds have received sexts and 4 percent have sent them.

With more receivers than senders, sexting has given rise to a new issue regarding sexual conduct and boundaries—the nonconsensual sext, which is received without request or sent without permission. To some observers, it may qualify as a

---

1. Quoted in Matthew Holehouse, "Woot! Retweet and Sexting Enter the Dictionary," *Telegraph*, August 18, 2011. http://www.telegraph.co.uk/culture/culturenews/8708448/Woot-Retweet-and-sexting-enter-the-dictionary.html.

form of sexual harassment, making those on the receiving end feel uncomfortable and embarrassed or intruded upon and violated. "The non-consensual sext is the equivalent of a guy you've had sex with randomly grabbing your boob at a party because he thinks since you gave yourself to him once or twice or five times that you belong to him . . . whenever he wants,"[2] claims Jessica Roy, editor of *Time* magazine's News-Feed. Why? "Because non-consensual sexting reveals a fundamental disrespect for women as people with thoughts and feelings and schedules that do not always line up with your arousal timetable. It turns women into blow-up dolls cradling iPhones," she continues. Out of respect, men (and women) should send an introductory message before firing off a nude photo, insists Roy: "After all, as with most things related to sex, it all comes down to communication—maybe both of you are into the surprise sext, but talking about it first is key."[3]

As far as privacy and policy are concerned, nonconsensual sexting takes on a different meaning; it is when the receiver forwards the message to others without consent of the sender. The common scenario occurs after a breakup, when an ex-boyfriend or ex-girlfriend shares a sext out of spite or vengeance. In response to incidents that have led to teen suicide and the unwilling exposure of individuals on "revenge porn" websites, lawmakers have sought to make it illegal. In December 2013, the state of Victoria in Australia outlawed the activity, and several bills have been introduced across the United States, including in California and Ohio, to prevent this type of nonconsensual texting. "When perpetrators misuse sexually suggestive or explicit messages or images to coerce or abuse, it can have an immediate and significant impact on a victim's life. Many sexting victims are revictimized in their school,

2. Jessica Roy, "Non-Consensual Sexting: The Hot New Way to Make Someone Really Uncomfortable," *Time*, April 25, 2014. http://time.com/77540/non-consensual-sexting-the-hot-new-way-to-make-someone-really-uncomfortable.
3. Ibid.

workplace or community,"[4] asserts the National Network to End Domestic Violence. The organization explains that considering "the speed with which sexts get shared, agencies working with victims of abusive or nonconsensual sexting need to be prepared to respond quickly" and "understand options and limitations for trying to remove sexts posted online."[5]

While enabled by advances in mobile technology, sexting is a deeply personal topic, concerning not only lust but sexual expression, love, and trust. "Sexting is not an IT [information technology] issue, it's a relationships issue,"[6] declares Sue Berkowitz, deputy children's commissioner for England. When sexting goes wrong, it is also a legal issue, and for some, even a constitutional one. *At Issue: Sexting* investigates the range of potential impacts and consequences for all individuals involved as well as what motivates people to bare it all in a text message.

4. National Network to End Domestic Violence, "Sexting," accessed April 28, 2014. http://nnedv.org/downloads/SafetyNet/OVW/NNEDV_Sexting_2011.pdf.

5. Ibid.

6. Quoted in BBC News, "'Sexting' Survey Shows Pressure Faced by Teens," October 16, 2013. http://www.bbc.com/news/uk-24539514.

1

The Dangers of Teen Sexting

Raychelle Cassada Lohmann

Based in South Carolina, Raychelle Cassada Lohmann is a school counselor and coauthor of The Bullying Workbook for Teens: Activities to Help You Deal with Social Aggression and Cyberbullying.

Sexting can have serious, lifelong consequences for teens. Defined as sending, receiving, or forwarding sexually explicit photos or messages through texts or e-mails, these sexual exchanges are instantaneous and more powerful than ever before; once a photo is sent, there is no control over who sees and shares it. Nonetheless, research shows that a high percentage of teens engage in sexting. Some may feel invincible and do it impulsively, while other adolescents may sext out of curiosity, because of peer pressure, or because they are in love. Sexting can take an emotional toll on teens if it leads to bullying and compromises their social and online reputations, in addition to resulting in legal ramifications.

Engaging in sexting is a dangerous activity for teens! It can have adverse side effects and the consequences can be lifelong. New research shows that approximately 20–30 percent of teens have sent and/or received a sext. Plus, according to research those teens who are sexting or propositioned to send a sext are more likely than their peers to have sexual intercourse. So, just what is sexting, who's doing it, why are they doing it, and what are the consequences? I'll attempt to answer those questions and more in this blog, "The Dangers of Teen Sexting."

What Is Sexting?

Sexting is sending, receiving, or forwarding sexual photos or sexually suggestive messages through text message or email. While the term "Sext" has been around since about 2005, the idea of exchanging or recording sexual material isn't a new concept. Historically sexual material has been distributed by means of: drawings, photographs, and videos. Then along came the internet through which electronic devices and social media outlets have changed the game of sexual exchanges. These modern technology advances have made sexual exchanges much easier and more powerful than ever before. With a click of a button a picture can be distributed to many people instantaneously—and once it's out there, there's no going back.

Researchers at the University of Texas Medical Branch found teens who "sext" may be more likely to engage in sexual behaviors.

Recent Research

Just recently there has been some interesting research released on teen sexting:

The first is from the University of Utah's Department of Psychology. Researchers surveyed 606 teens ages 14–18 and found that approximately 20 percent of the teens said they had sent a sexual image of themselves via cell phone. About twice as many teens admitted to receiving a sext. To top it off, of those who reported receiving a sext, well over 25 percent said that they had forwarded it to someone else. So, they're sharing the pics with their friends.

Sadly a third of the teens stated that they didn't think about the legal ramifications or consequences of their actions. And this may come as no surprise, teens who engaged in sexting were more likely than others to find the activity acceptable. They had "justified" their behavior to the point that they didn't view it as wrong. That's scary.

The second study was published in the *Archives of Pediatric & Adolescent Medicine*. Researchers at the University of Texas Medical Branch found teens who "sext" may be more likely to engage in sexual behaviors. Here are some of the findings:

- 28% of teens admitted to having sent a sext.

- 76.2% of teens who were propositioned to sext admitted to having had sexual intercourse.

- Girls were asked to send a sext (68%) more often than boys (42%).

- The peak age of sexting is around 16 and 17 years of age.

- Sexting seems to decline in individuals 18 and older.

Why Are They Doing It?

They may be curious. . . .

Sex creates curiosity, which leads to exploration and experimentation—especially with teens. This is not a new thing and it's completely normal. Teens may be curious as to what others look like naked and also easily aroused by nudity.

They may be pressured. . . .

Peer pressure to participate in sex could be another reason teens are succumbing to sending racy pics of themselves.

Think about it:

If you're a guy and your friends all have sexual photos of girls on their phones, you may feel pressured to do the same; especially if your "guy" friends single you out if you don't.

On the flip side, if you're a girl and other girls are boasting about sending pictures to their boyfriends you may feel you need to do the same; especially if you feel like "everyone else is doing it."

They may be in love. . . .

Remember your first love? To the love-stricken teen it's easy to cave to the pressure when you think "this is the one." You believe with all of your heart this is the person you're destined to be with for eternity. Dramatic, yeah, but remember those teen years? To you this person is trustworthy and you would do anything, and I mean anything, for them. To the teen who's in need of this type of attention or in need of love and acceptance, he/she may give in and do something he'll/she'll later regret.

Emotionally sexting can take a toll on a person, especially if it backfires and gets into the wrong hands.

They may not be thinking. . . .

There's a special part of the brain called the prefrontal cortex (aka the CEO [chief executive officer] of the brain) that is responsible for problem solving, impulse control, and weighing out options. Unfortunately for teens, this area of the brain is not fully developed. In fact, it doesn't fully mature until the early to mid-twenties. So, while we expect our teens to know better, the fact is there are some physiological reasons teens think they're invincible.

What Are the Emotional and Legal Consequences?

Emotionally

Emotionally sexting can take a toll on a person, especially if it backfires and gets into the wrong hands. Teens have a unique ability to feel like they're invincible. So, even though they may know that sexting is wrong, they don't think they're going to get caught.

Another emotional catch is that sexting may lead to bullying for the teen whose photos have been solicited to others. This creates a harsh world for a teen to live. Oftentimes they don't reach out for help because of embarrassment and disappointment, fear of making it worse, or fear of getting into trouble. To many teens they may feel like they're caught in a trap with no way out.

Also, sexting can compromise reputations. Not just social reputations but digital reputations can take a hit. Once a photo is out, there's no way of knowing how many people have saved it, tagged it, shared it, etc. Unfortunately the photo could re-surface years after it was taken and posted. Plus, more and more college reps and prospective employers are seeking information about candidates and they're doing this online. What they find online could sway their decision about whether or not the person lands the job or gets accepted into the school of his/her dreams.

Legally

Sadly, laws lag behind technology . . . but here is the good news: In 2011, 21 U.S. states passed legislation related to sexting. In 2012, at least 13 states so far are considering bills or resolutions aimed at "sexting."

How Do You Protect Your Teen?

It's important that parents spend time speaking with their teens about sex. Young people need to know that it's okay to have desires and feelings. Talk to your teens about the impact and consequences of acting out sexual desires and how they can stay true to their morals, values and beliefs when faced with adversity. Also, discuss the consequences of acting out sexually (pregnancy, STDs, etc.). Please don't treat sex as a taboo topic in your household; rather, create a safe environment for your teen to ask questions and have an open dialogue. Awkward? Yeah at first it may feel awkward to you and your teen to discuss sex, but don't let that keep you from having the discussion. The more you talk, the easier it'll become and the weirdness will begin to wear off.

It is important that parents are in the loop with what their teens are doing with technology. So many things have Wi-Fi access nowadays. Devices such as personal computers, video game consoles, hand held gaming devices, Smartphones, tablets, e-readers and even digital audio players can connect to a network and create an opportunity for a teen to make a poor decision. Technology has pros and cons. Unfortunately, some of the cons carry some hefty consequences.

In conclusion, with 20-30 percent of today's teens sexting it is important that we educate our teens on the dangers associated with it. On the brighter side, we still have about 70-80 percent of teens making good decisions when it comes to sexting. In my experience as a counselor one of the things that I love to hear from a teen is "I have a good relationship with my parents." or "I can tell my mom/dad anything." That's an awesome statement to hear from a teen. Parents, please reach out to your teens and create an environment that allows them to let you into their life. . . .

2

Sexting Among Teens Can Be Harmful

Katie Abbondanza

Katie Abbondanza is a senior editor at Girls' Life.

A recent study showed that of the nearly one thousand teens surveyed, almost 30 percent had sent a sext, and almost 60 percent had been asked to send a revealing photo of themselves. As an act of rebellion or the result of peer pressure or bullying, sexting has become more prevalent among teens. What is not taken into account by young women when they naively send images of themselves to boyfriends and others is the humiliation, loss of control, depression, and even possible criminal charges that can result. Sending a sext can start a scary chain reaction, but teens need to know that they don't have to deal with the consequences alone, and help is avalable.

When Allyson Pereira was a sophomore in high school, she sent a naked picture of herself to her then-boyfriend. The pair broke up, and he forwarded her very intimate photo to his entire contact list. The picture went viral, flying from phone to phone until untold numbers of people in her New Jersey town—and beyond—had seen her totally exposed.

"Mostly, I was just humiliated," Allyson, now 22, says of the experience. "I was ashamed because I had never been that kind of person. It was embarrassing knowing my teachers had seen it. Even my brother got the picture forwarded to him."

She was bullied—badly—but felt like she couldn't speak up because back then the laws in New Jersey were worded so that she could have been charged as a sex offender for sending the pornographic snap in the first place.

"It was considered a worse crime than actually forwarding my picture," she says, admitting that her life was turned completely upside down after the incident. "It was really hard. I had one friend who truly stuck by me through it all. She was there to talk to me and walk me down the halls and be that shoulder for me. That really saved my life."

Girls who get involved with taking, sending and forwarding these kinds of inappropriate pictures can get themselves into deeper trouble—both emotional and legal—than they might realize.

Allyson isn't exaggerating—she attempted suicide during that awful time. And, sadly, her story isn't unique. According to a study done by the Education Development Center in Massachusetts, there's a scary link between sexting and depression and suicide.

"What we found is that teens who are involved in sexting are two times as likely to show depressive symptoms," says EDC researcher Shari Kessel Schneider. Teens who swapped suggestive pictures were more likely to have attempted suicide in the last year as well.

"We don't know if the sexting is causing these feelings or whether kids who are feeling sad or hopeless might be more likely to engage in sexting," Schneider admits.

What is known, though, is that girls who get involved with taking, sending and forwarding these kinds of inappropriate pictures can get themselves into deeper trouble—both emotional and legal—than they might realize.

Not Just "Bad Girls"

A 2012 study published in the journal *Pediatrics & Adolescent Medicine* showed that nearly 30 percent of the 948 teens surveyed had sexted and nearly 60 percent of teens had been asked to send a revealing image.

While lots of girls say no, many are feeling pressure to sext—and then are being bullied or tormented once they've sent snaps. The truth is, as soon as you hit "send" on a risky photo, you're putting yourself in major jeopardy.

"Don't forget how many people are going to see that picture," says Dr. Stephanie Mihalas, a licensed psychologist who works with kids and teens. If you send a picture to one guy, simply assume his entire list of contacts will get more than a glimpse. There are countless ways those revealing pictures could circulate, even if your crush or BF [boyfriend] seems trustworthy.

Almost 90 percent of suggestive photographs posted on social media sites wind up on pornographic websites.

Consider the sexting ring in Vermont, where a group of guys asked girls for pictures and then, it turned out, shared all the photos they received in a group e-mail account. That's at least a dozen boys, if not more, who saw those girls naked. Who knows how many people they forwarded the private images to before finally getting caught?

And then there's the grim tale of the eighth-grader in the Midwest who sent a naked shot to a guy she liked. According to *The New York Times*, it was forwarded and wound up in the hands of a not-so-nice girl. She then sent it to her contact list with the caption, "Ho alert! If you think this girl is a whore, then text this to all your friends." The picture continued to circulate, though the two perpetrators were eventually caught.

Although some picture-sending services swear your image disappears after just a few seconds, there's really no telling what will happen once it gets in a guy's hands. He could say he's alone at home and really be out with a group of friends. Or maybe he'll use his buddy's phone to take a picture of the snap you sent, meaning it won't vanish after a few seconds.

And keep in mind it's not just your BF's basketball team who might get a glimpse: A recent study by the Internet Watch Foundation revealed that almost 90 percent of suggestive photographs posted on social media sites wind up on pornographic websites. Bottom line? Once they're out, there's no telling how many people might view them or who might contact you about them.

When Sexting Leads to Bullying

Sexting has ushered in the next generation of bullying, making girls who expose themselves online particularly vulnerable to predators of all kinds. Say a girl's BF asks for a revealing picture. Immediately, the manipulation and power struggle can start, even if a girl says no way.

Take Quinn L., 15, for example. A boy texted her, asking her to send him something revealing. "I said no right off the bat," she says. "And then he was like, 'But it's nothing bad!'"

Once you start sending pictures—even one—you lose control of the image and some of your power in the relationship.

That kind of pressure is a common type of bullying, but that doesn't mean you should cave in.

"A boy might tell you, 'If you don't do this, this isn't going to work out,' or 'You don't really love me,'" says Dr. Mihalas. That's a total power play that might make a girl question herself, wondering if she's being too prudish or if she'll lose her boyfriend if she refuses to sext.

Dr. Mihalas adds that it's not just guys who are influencing girls to share provocative pictures—some girls who send scandalous images are doing it to rebel against parents who tell them not to or because other girls around them are also sexting.

Once you start sending pictures—even one—you lose control of the image and some of your power in the relationship. Your boyfriend might want to see more and threaten consequences if you don't keep them coming.

"It can become a real victim/prey mentality," says Dr. Mihalas, and the intensity of it all can be overwhelming.

Sexting Gets Even More Serious

"I can never get that photo back." Those are the haunting words Amanda Todd held up before a camera and posted on YouTube in September 2012. A month later, the 16-year-old Canadian teen was found dead in her bedroom—an apparent suicide.

A few years earlier, Amanda had been in an online video chat, where she was asked to flash her chest. She did. Amanda probably thought just the people in the chat room would see, but someone captured the image and held onto it.

The predator used the picture to blackmail and torment Amanda, threatening to send the image to her friends. Eventually, he did. She was bullied and ostracized at school, and ultimately had to change schools. She turned to cutting, drinking and drugs. And then, she took her life.

Yes, this is a worst-case scenario. But the point is, it happens. And Amanda's story is a harsh reminder of the scary chain reaction that sending just one sext can cause.

Surviving a Sext

So what should you do if you send a text that goes viral? First off, get help from a trusted adult, like a school counselor or a close relative.

"You can't deal with it alone, as much as you might think you can," Allyson says. "High school isn't the rest of your life—it will get better."

Also, know that you have rights. Although Allyson initially felt paralyzed by her situation, she eventually faced it head-on, even telling her story on MTV News' Sexting In America: When Privates Go Public.

She also wrote to legislators to get sexting laws in New Jersey changed—the very laws that kept her from speaking out when her naked picture got into the hands of her classmates and neighbors.

Sexting laws vary from state to state, but in some places, having naked photos on your phone can count as child pornography, which is a seriously big deal with long-term consequences.

Now Allyson is an anti-bullying advocate who speaks to teens about the dangers of sexting. She also has a powerful message for you: "Don't feel like you have to show him your body to get him to like you. If he really liked you, he wouldn't be asking for a picture."

3

Sexting Among Teens Is Not Always Harmful

Anne Collier

Based in northern California, Anne Collier is editor of NetFamilyNews.org and codirector of ConnectSafely.org, a website and forum that provides information on youths and the Internet.

To some teens, the term "sexting" to describe sending and receiving nude photos on smartphones can be alienating because it treats the activity as a deviant or criminal behavior. But a new area of research contextualizes sexting beyond crime, viewing it as an experimental or consensual act between teens. Indeed, sexting may involve a broad spectrum of motivations, such as pushing boundaries in "Truth or Dare" games, to bond and identify within a group, and as part of flirting or foreplay. Also, it may be used to connect in long-distance relationships; to guard the safety of closeted lesbian, gay, bisexual, and transgender individuals; and to abstain from actual physical contact for cultural or religious reasons. To better guide young people, adults must understand these motivations and recognize that sexting is not always harmful.

Despite what we see in news headlines, there is no single term that people who share nude photos use, according to Australian researcher and author Nina Funnell, who has interviewed some four dozen 16- to 25-year-olds about it. Especially not "sexting," she said in a talk I got to hear in Sydney this spring (their fall [in 2013]). Using the term tends to alienate young people, she said. And there are many more *motivations* for "sexting," as adults have come to call it, than there are terms for it. More on that in a moment—first a bit of background. . . .

Until 2011, when Janis Wolak and David Finkelhor at the University of New Hampshire published the first typology of sexting, it was seen and treated as a single undifferentiated and mainly illegal practice. Wolak and Finkelhor significantly advanced understanding of the practice when they created two categories of "youth-produced sexual images"—"Aggravated" and "Experimental"—based on their review of "550 cases obtained from a national survey of law enforcement agencies." The cases all involved "images of minors created by minors that could qualify as child pornography under applicable criminal statutes."

We need to understand sexting better in the context of sexual health and adolescent development, including healthy risk-taking.

This was a major step forward because 1) it opened up thought to the idea that sexting isn't just deviant or criminal behavior and 2) it opened up "experimental" or consensual sexting as an important new area of study. Still, it's helpful to note that Wolak and Finkelhor's study was of sexting cases that involved *law enforcement*, which both makes it all the more significant that the "experimental" category emerged and makes it all the more important to understand that category better (and possibly rename it) by studying it outside the context of criminal law.

Out of the Crime Context

I'd say the next step in our collective understanding of sexting was psychology professor Elizabeth Englander's finding that much of the harmful kind of sexting is coercive, and "any discussion of coercive sexting should be made in the context of sexual harassment," she reported in a study she published last year—so we need to educate young people about what sexual harassment is in the digital age so they can protect themselves better not just from prosecution or a betrayal of trust but also from sexual harassment and manipulation.

But it's equally important for parents and educators to understand that not all sexting is harmful—or even experimental. More and more, it's also just the latest way people of all ages use imagery in consensual sexual activity. So we need to understand sexting better in the context of sexual health and adolescent development, including healthy risk-taking.

Sexual Health and Healthy Risk-taking

So now the vital next phase: Nina is one of the researchers doing the important work of filling in the picture on the "experimental" side (though she found the word to be problematic) through interviews with people who engage in it. She's talking with teens and adults mostly ages 16–25, but some older ("into their 60s"), she said, "both male and female, and a mix of heterosexual, bisexual and same-sex-attracted." This qualitative research will go into a book she's working on.

What she has found is that sexting involves a broad spectrum of motivations. "Based on my interviews with young people, I've found that the range of motives around sexting is as complex and multifaceted as you would expect to find in relation to any other sexual activity," Nina wrote me in an email after her talk, and not all the motivations are sexual, she added.

The Motivation Spectrum

Among the motivations she's heard from interviewees are: "pushing boundaries" (in games like "Truth or Dare"); "group identity bonding (sharing images in a group as a 'trust game' in order to develop a sense of group solidarity)"; "testing out one's desirability or sexual power with either a stranger or a prospective partner"; flirting, foreplay (turned up by Pew Internet in 2009), or a purely digital sexual activity in its own right [in person or online]; a way for partners in a long-distance relationship to stay connected; safety for LGBT [lesbian, gay, bisexual, transgender] partners who haven't yet come out; and safety for cultural or religious reasons (when physical contact is not allowed before marriage).

The adults in [teens'] lives will be much better-equipped to guide them if we understand that practices such as sexting aren't single undifferentiated new "threats" but rather spectrums of tech-related behaviors.

"We shouldn't ever make assumptions about why a young person might engage in a particular behavior, because their reasons are highly diverse and individual," Nina wrote. They can also be highly localized.

Why Better Understanding Helps

"In a particular school, you might get one particular group of 8–10 boys who all share nude images of girls without consent as a way of 'bonding' [what Wolak and Finkelhor would probably call 'aggravated sexting'] and, while that is accepted within their micro group, meanwhile the rest of the students [in their class] are dead opposed to it." [She's talking about the overall protective social norms of the larger community (which deserve acknowledgment and support from adults) around an anti-social group dynamic).]

"That sort of thing to me demonstrates how values and 'unwritten rules' are negotiated at a very, very localized level," Nina added, pointing to the challenge of educators: that "top-down approaches would be unlikely to generate much behavioral change for those 8–10 individuals." By "top-down approaches," she's referring to general anti-sexting campaigns and directives from authorities. "The spectrum of motivations must be better understood before we can develop meaningful educational resources," she wrote.

The vast majority of teens already have plenty of positive social norms in place—norms they've been exposed to all their lives, starting in their families and practiced at school, online, wherever they interact. The adults in their lives will be much better-equipped to guide them if we understand that practices such as sexting aren't single undifferentiated new "threats" but rather spectrums of tech-related behaviors just as affected by social norms as social experiences that have nothing to do with technology. And we'll also be much better able to guide them—and to enlist their help when problems arise—if we acknowledge and support the intelligent norms and values they are already practicing.

A little more on the researcher I feature in this post: Nina Funnell was awarded the Australian Human Rights Commission award in 2010 and was a finalist for Young Australian of The Year for her work in sexual violence prevention. She contributed to the book *Big Porn Inc: Exposing the Harms of the Global Pornography Industry* and is currently working on a book about sexting.

4

Teens Sext to Experiment Sexually and Socialize Independently

Sean Carton

Sean Carton is a professor at the University of Baltimore's School of Communications and chief creative officer at idfive, an advertising and design agency.

For teens, the impact of mobile technology and social media is similar to the changes brought on by the automobile: it offers them a place away from adult supervision, where they can interact with each other with unprecedented freedom. As with the backseat of a car, a smartphone allows teens to explore their sexuality through sexting and to socialize independently. In fact, sexting, online dating, and video chat are transforming how young people come together, changing courtship into a more casual and sexually permissive activity with low risks, costs, and commitments. Needing immediacy and connection, the "Connected Generation" is less formal, freer in experimentation and play, fixated on images rather than texts, and highly open with and trusting of their social networks.

We are in the midst of a generational change driven by technology just as profound as the one that happened when teens and cars began to come together in the 1920's. But while the last big shift was being driven by advances in transportation, this one is being driven by advances in communication.

The Automobile's Impact on the American Teenager

Prior to the popularization of the automobile, human families were usually made up of two groups: children who lived at home under the watchful eyes (and rules) of their parents and adults who'd split off to form their own families or seek their own fortunes out in the world. It wasn't until the automobile came along and gave children the independence to get around in the world without their parents, the freedom to go pretty much wherever they wanted to go, and the privacy to do what they wanted to do away from the watchful eyes of adults that the concept of *teenager* arose. In addition . . . the increased mobility brought about by automobiles also led to the development of consolidated high schools that drew from a wide geographic area, high schools which also served as a place for a unique teen culture to develop.

> *It's not hard to see the similarities between the impact of automobile culture on young people and the changes occurring as a result of mobile and social media.*

Examining the evolution of courtship is probably one of the best ways to understand the far-reaching impact of the automobile on human relationships. Prior to the automobile young people "courted" under the watchful gaze of their parents in the home or public gatherings, rarely (if ever) enjoying more than a few minutes alone. As soon as the car comes along, home-based courtship quickly became automobile-based dating where amorous teens could enjoy nights out away from their parents, often gathering together with their peers at locations friendly to teens. And since the car offered an unheard of opportunity for privacy, it also became possible for teens to experiment with sex in a way they never had had the opportunity to explore before while courting on the front porch.

The impact of the car on the American teenager was enormous. Whole new categories of businesses arose to cater to the newly-freed teen. Drive-in restaurants. Drive-in movies. "Dates" as special events involving only the young couple. Suburbs (and, later, suburban teenage angst). Malls. Teen fashion. Entire genres of film. While rock-and-roll may have developed without the automobile, the big-production stadium rock of the 60's and 70's (not to mention festivals like Woodstock) wouldn't have been possible without young people having the ability to go where they wanted to, when they wanted to, with whomever they wanted to. And it's pretty hard to imagine the Sexual Revolution occurring if it had to happen on Mom and Pop's front porch.

The automobile created "teen culture" by providing a means for kids of a certain age to exercise their desire for independence, privacy, and mobility. It also helped them develop a sense of identity separate from their parents and closer connections with their peers. It helped them to become more confident by providing a means for controlling their own lives . . . as even if for only a brief period of time and only if their parents would let them borrow the family car.

The Very Real and Separate Place of Social Media

Looking at social media today it's not hard to see the similarities between the impact of automobile culture on young people and the changes occurring as a result of mobile and social media. Even if teens can't use social media to physically "go" anywhere, it has created a very real and separate "place" that's even farther away from the watchful gaze of adults than the drive-in theaters, malls, and "Lover's Lanes" of the past. In the virtual world of social media teens feel free to interact with unprecedented independence, privacy (at least from their parents), and control where they can experiment with forming their own identities, explore their sexuality, and maintain a constant connection with their "real-life" friends in a way that blurs the boundaries between "real life" and cyberspace.

Just as the introduction of the automobile changed teen courtship and arguably had a big role in the later sexual revolution, social media . . . is having a huge impact on how young people get together today.

While teenagers of the past may have been granted brief periods of independence in their cars, they eventually had to come home. Today's teen—especially if equipped with a smartphone—may never physically leave home but instead is now able to mentally "leave home" by connecting with their peers in social media no matter where they may be in the "real world." Social media now serves as a very real, very accessible, and very powerful "alternate universe" that young people can escape to whenever and wherever they want. Whether at home, school or family outings . . . as long as they have more than a bar or two on their phones, they're able to virtually "get away" whenever they want.

If you doubt the effects that this change is having on the lives of those who have grown up in the age of the Internet and social media, consider that more and more teens are waiting longer to drive: in 1983 69% of 17 year-olds had drivers licenses . . . in 2008 that number had dropped to 50%. Facebook opened its doors to high school students in 2005.

And just as the introduction of the automobile changed teen courtship and arguably had a big role in the later sexual revolution, social media (especially mobile social media) is having a huge impact on how young people get together today. In January of 2013 the *New York Times* asked whether or not we'd reached "The End of Courtship" citing the increasing acceptance of casual sex in the "hookup culture" and the move from dating to casually "hanging out." The article also looks at several experts who've studied online dating and found that the ready availability of potential mates met via social networking or online dating services has lead to an increasingly popular "shot-gun" approach of casual, low-cost, low-risk, and low-commitment meetups between people interested in dating. As one 20-something quoted in the *Times* article points out, "It's like online job applications, you can target many people simultaneously—it's like darts on a dart board, eventually one will stick." We're a long way from when a "first date" meant bringing someone home for a "parlor sit" with Mother and Father.

No Separation Between "Real Life" and Online Life

The social media revolution is still young, but it's clearly having a profound impact on younger users who have never known a world without it. To the social media generation there's no separation between "real life" and online life . . . it's just all "life." There are no discrete and separate segments: whether they're at home, at school, at work, or away with the family on vacation they're still connected and communicating with their friends. If things are going badly in one place—being physically bullied in school, for example—it continues in a different format online (e.g. cyberbullying). Rather than leave one group of friends when graduating high school and going to college, social media allows young people to continue those connections, perhaps to the exclusion of new ones at their new school. New tools that provide greater opportunities for non-verbal communication (Tumblr, SnapChat, and Vine, for example) further increase the feeling of "connection" by allowing users to seem to share in the same experiences as their friends through photos and videos. While they're not really "there," they're there.

For marketers reaching out to teens, it's vital that we understand that teens today aren't just different because of the kind of fashion they wear or the kind of music they listen to. Today's teens who've grown up never knowing what it's like to not be connected are as profoundly different from teenagers of just a decade ago as teenagers of the 1950's and 60's were from teens in the Victorian era.

Just as the car gave teenagers a platform on which to physically assert their independence and identities, social media provides a platform on which to mentally assert the same things.

To reach them, it's vital to recognize their need for immediacy and connection. They're used to being connected 24/7 and don't understand why a text or a message on Facebook sent at 3AM might not get answered until noon the next day. They live in a world where experimentation and play are the norm and don't see why everyone shouldn't be free to experiment with new things . . . is it any wonder why The Dark Knight's Joker's query "Why so serious?" has continued to resonate throughout social media? They're informal and don't see the need for formality but are, in fact, a little intimidated by alien-seeming adults (even while they may come off as comfortable because of their informality). They also don't understand inflexibility when it comes to deadlines, meeting times, or even specific locations; after all, if you're connected and your friends are connected then why not change where you're going to meet (or what time) on a whim? Everyone will know about the change pretty much instantaneously, right? And if they don't get the message, well, who'd want to hang out with a disconnected loser anyway?

The Connected Generation

The Connected Generation wants less text and more images (or amusing combinations of the two). They are at once protective of the boundaries of their "tribe" and are wary of anyone trying to break into their network (advertisers, that's you!) but, at the same time, are incredibly open with those they trust and accept because their boundaries between "public" and "private" have become so blurred as to be irrelevant. They want to be independent and make their own way in the world, but struggle with decisions and often turn to their networks for advice and affirmation. And if you aren't on board with (and willing to use) the channels they're using to communicate, you might as well just send a telegram.

The introduction of the automobile into American culture changed many things, but it particularly changed the lives of teenagers by giving them the independence, privacy, control, mobility, and connections that they'd always wanted. Just as the car gave teenagers a platform on which to physically assert their independence and identities, social media provides a platform on which to mentally assert the same things, even while their lives in the "real world" remain (on the surface) only marginally different from the teens that came before them. Tumblr, Facebook, and Google+ are the soda fountains, parking lots, and fast-food hangouts of the Age of Social media. YouTube and Vine its drive-in movies. And sexting and anonymous video chat services are the new back seat.

5

"Sexting" Bullying Cited in Teen's Suicide

Michael Inbar

Michael Inbar is a former contributor to Today.com, the website of the Today Show.

Sexting, or electronically transmitting sexual messages or images, is linked to cases of bullying and suicide among youths. In 2009, Hope Witsell, a thirteen-year-old from Florida, hanged herself after being taunted and teased by her peers for sending a boy a photo of her exposed breasts—which was widely disseminated— and suspended from school. Despite support from her friends and tough love from her parents, Witsell gave into peer pressure and sexted again before she committed suicide. Entries in her journal revealed deep emotional suffering from bullying. According-ing to an expert on Internet safety, it is upstanding teens from good homes who feel the most guilt for sexting and the most pain from the bullying that follows.

Hope Witsell was just beginning the journey from child to teen. The middle-school student had a tight-knit group of friends, the requisite poster of "Twilight" heartthrob Robert Pattinson and big plans to become a landscaper when she grew up.

But one impetuous move robbed Hope of her childhood, and eventually, her life. The 13-year-old Florida girl sent a topless photo of herself to a boy in hope of gaining his attention. Instead, she got the attention of her school, as well as the high school nearby.

The incessant bullying by classmates that followed when the photo spread put an emotional weight upon Hope that she ultimately could not bear.

Hope Witsell hanged herself in her bedroom 11 weeks ago.

Her death is only the second known case of a suicide linked to bullying after "sexting"—the practice of transmitting sexual messages or images electronically. In March, 18-year-old Jesse Logan killed herself in the face of a barrage of taunts when an ex-boyfriend forwarded explicit photos of her following their split.

Hope Witsell's grieving mother, Donna Witsell, is now coming forward to offer a cautionary story in hope of sparing others to the loss she endures. Appearing on TODAY Wednesday with attorney Parry Aftab, a leading Internet safety expert, Witsell told Meredith Vieira how her daughter's life, once so promising, unraveled after one mistake.

Hope got involved in a dangerous, all-too-typical teen game. . . . It's an act that is becoming more and more commonplace among teens.

The Witsells, from the small rural suburb of Sundance, Fla., are a churchgoing family. Donna admitted to Vieira she knew little to nothing about "sexting" before her daughter's drama, but she and her husband, Charlie, tried to teach Hope and Donna's three children from previous relationships right from wrong in the cyberworld.

"As far as training them on the Internet and what to look at and what not to look at, yeah, we talked about it," Witsell told Vieira.

But Hope got involved in a dangerous, all-too-typical teen game. In June, at the end of her seventh-grade year at Beth

Shields Middle School, she sent a picture of her exposed breasts to a boy she liked. It's an act that is becoming more and more commonplace among teens (a poll recently showed some 20 percent of teens admitting they've sent nude pictures of themselves over cell phones).

But a third party intercepted the photo while using the boy's cell phone, and soon, not only had many of the school's students gawked at the picture, but students at the local high school and even neighboring schools were ogling it.

While Hope's photo spread, her friends rallied around her in the midst of incessant taunting and vulgar remarks thrown Hope's way. Friends told the *St. Petersburg Times*, which originally chronicled Hope's story, that they literally surrounded Hope as she walked the hallways while other students shouted "whore" and "slut" at her.

"The hallways were not fun at that time—she'd walk into class and somebody would say, 'Oh, here comes the slut,'" Hope's friend, Lane James, told the newspaper.

Clearly, the taunts were getting to Hope. In a journal entry discovered after her death, Hope wrote, "Tons of people talk about me behind my back and I hate it because they call me a whore! And I can't be a whore. I'm too inexperienced. So secretly, TONS of people hate me."

Shortly after the school year ended, school officials caught wind of the hubbub surrounding Hope's cell phone photo. They contacted the Witsells and told them Hope would be suspended for the first week of the next school year.

Donna Witsell told Vieira that she and her husband practiced tough love on Hope, grounding her for the summer and suspending her cell phone and computer privileges.

Choking up with tears, Witsell told Vieira, "She received her punishment for a mistake she'd made. You set rules and boundaries in the household. . . . You punish them and then you let it go. You love them. You continue to talk with them, you continue to try to keep that line of communication open, but most of all you continue to love them. You don't shame them."

Still, Hope had a very trying summer. A student adviser for the local Future Farmers of America chapter, Hope was allowed by her parents to attend the FFA convention in Orlando. But in a display of just how prevalent teen pressure is when it comes to "sexting," Hope gave in to incessant badgering from a group of boys staying across from Hope and her friend in a hotel room to provide them with a picture of her breasts.

Mounting Pressure

The downward spiral of Hope's life was unstoppable. When she returned to school this fall after serving her suspension, the school informed her she could no longer serve as a student adviser to the FFA. She finally admitted to her parents the abuse she was taking.

On Sept. 11, Hope met with school counselors, who noticed cuts on Hope's leg they believed to be self-inflicted. They had her sign a "no-harm contract," in which she promised to talk to an adult if she felt the urge to hurt herself. But, attorney Aftab told TODAY, the school didn't inform Hope's parents of the contract. "In this case, the school blew it," Aftab said. "They never told the parents how at risk she was."

The following day, Hope wrote in her journal: "I'm done for sure now. I can feel it in my stomach. I'm going to try and strangle myself. I hope it works."

Donna Witsell went to Hope's bedroom to give her a kiss goodnight. She was met with the most horrifying scene any parent could face.

"It was as if she was standing right there in front of me," Witsell told NBC News. "Her head was hanging down. I said, 'Hope, what are you doing?' And then I realized there was a scarf around her neck."

Hope had knotted one end of a pink scarf around the canopy of her bed and the other around her neck. She was taken by ambulance to a local hospital, where she was pronounced dead.

Attorney Aftab is at the forefront of highlighting the very real dangers of "sexting" among the teen set. And even though Hope was incredibly young for sexual behavior, a Harris Poll shows up to 9 percent of 13-year-old girls admit they have sent nude pictures of themselves on cell phones.

Aftab, who held Donna Witsell's hand throughout the trying TODAY interview, told Vieira it's often upstanding children growing up in good homes who have the biggest propensity to feel guilt over their sexual actions, and most feel the stings of the bullying that comes afterward.

"Good kids are the ones this is happening to; Jesse was a great kid, and now we have Hope," she said. "Good kids; they're the ones who are committing suicide when a picture like this gets out."

6

Sexting Among Teens Should Not Be Criminalized

American Civil Liberties Union

Headquartered in New York City, the American Civil Liberties Union (ACLU) is a nonprofit national organization that works in the courts, legislatures, and communities to protect individual rights.

Sexting among teens should not be criminalized. Current child pornography laws are designed to protect children, but when applied to sexting and teens, it subjects youths to potential felony charges, which can ruin their lives by labeling them as sex offenders and confusing them with adults convicted of heinous sex crimes against minors. In fact, adolescents can be charged as sex offenders for disseminating their own photos, which punishes the victim and those who carelessly share sexts from their significant others. It is recommended that teens are exempt from these criminal charges and procedures—including misdemeanors—and instead educated about responsible behavior and the need to respect privacy.

Sexting is the phenomenon of taking, sending, receiving or displaying nude images via cell phone, email, blog or other online communication. It is so common that according to a 2009 study by the National Campaign to Prevent Teen and Unplanned Pregnancy, one in five teens admitted to sexting.

American Civil Liberties Union, "Sexting: A Civil Liberties Briefing from the ACLU," ACLU Ohio Sexting Position Sheet, 2011. Copyright © 2011 American Civil Liberties Union of Ohio Foundation. All rights reserved. Reprinted with permission.

Prosecutions Are Too Varied

Prosecutors have broad discretion to decide how to charge young people with sexting, or whether to prosecute them at all. Current laws were not written with sexting in mind and provide no guidance. They might pursue felony convictions, which label the young person as a sex offender and carry mandatory registration requirements. Or they may charge a young person with misdemeanors without registration requirements, or impose hours of community service, or they may decide not to pursue charges at all.

Current Law

Currently in Ohio, sexting may result in two potential felony charges. The first is a violation of Ohio Revised Code section 2907.322, "Pandering Sexually Oriented Matter Involving a Minor," which is a fourth-degree felony. The other is a violation of Ohio Revised Code section 2907.323, "Illegal Use of Minor in Nudity Oriented Material or Performance." The degree of the felony conviction depends on whether someone transfers material (second degree), consents to photographing (fourth degree), or possesses or views the material (fifth degree). If convicted with the second or fourth degree felony a mandatory prison term will be imposed.

Furthermore, the federal Adam Walsh Act may label teens who send, receive or even share the photos as sex offenders. This will require the teens to register with law enforcement for decades, if not for life, after the completion of their sentence. If the conviction falls under the second or third tier of sex offender registration crimes, then the teens will be subjected to mandatory community notification (accessible by Internet). As a devastating result, these teens will be easily confused with adults convicted of rape, gross sexual imposition and other heinous sex crimes against children.

Child Pornography Laws Are Designed to Protect Children

The text and legislative intent of current laws aim to prevent adults from taking advantage of children. Under current law, a young person could be charged as a sex offender for disseminating their own picture. As a result, the victims may be the ones punished. In addition, these laws may be used against children who foolishly circulate pictures of their significant other. While this is inappropriate, it goes against the foundations of justice to ruin a young person's life because of one careless and immature action. Current legislation does not accurately address sexting, and the convictions under these codes are inappropriate for minors.

Child pornography laws were designed to protect one group, child victims, from others who do them harm. Sexting only has one group involved in the act, the children themselves.

Proposed Sexting Bills

Several bills were proposed in the Ohio General Assembly in 2010 to address sexting. The bills come up short because they still treat sexting behavior as a crime. However, they would reduce sexting to a misdemeanor and would not label the teens as sex offenders.

In 2011, Rep. Ron Maag (R-Lebanon) introduced House Bill 53, which was nearly identical to bills proposed in 2010.

The American Civil Liberties Union (ACLU) Position on Proposed Bills

Although both pending bills are designed specifically to address sexting as opposed to other acts and have reduced the criminal penalties to a misdemeanor, the ACLU opposes criminalizing sexting altogether. Child pornography laws were designed to protect one group, child victims, from others who do them harm. Sexting only has one group involved in the act, the children themselves. Since the bills specifically do not make a distinction between the victim and the offender, the victim is ultimately being punished for his/her acts.

ACLU Recommendations

The ACLU advocates the non-criminalization of teen sexting.

Laws are designed to protect victims from offenders, but attempts to criminalize sexting blur those lines.

· Existing criminal laws, that carry the potential for a felony conviction and sex offender restrictions, are not meant to address teen sexting. Under the existing laws and their extensive punitive effects, these teens will be stripped of a future as their education and work prospects will be bleak. These offenses currently impose a ban on living within 1,000 feet of schools and day care facilities. The ultimate impact of such convictions can ruin a teen's life.

Furthermore, the traditional role of juvenile courts supports rehabilitation of child offenders by keeping court records and proceedings confidential. This is substantially undermined by the current state of child pornography laws when applied to sexting. The juvenile court, under current laws, will not be able to continue to limit the public stigma experienced by child offenders.

While the sexting bills proposed do make a positive step in that they at least remove felony charges and sex offender labeling, they continue to treat adolescent behavior as a crime. Laws are designed to protect victims from offenders, but attempts to criminalize sexting blur those lines.

Certainly teens need to be taught responsible behavior, and how to respect their own and others' privacy. But that should be done by education, not threatening young people with criminal charges. Instead, current criminal offenses should be clarified to exempt adolescents who take, send and receive nude photos. In addition, current laws should exempt sexting adolescents from the Adam Walsh Act requirements. Schools should be encouraged to adopt curricula to teach young people how to use telecommunications responsibly.

There are other legal avenues to address sending or sharing private photos against someone's wishes, such as when a sexting recipient resends the photo in question to others who were not intended to see it. Tort laws provide a mechanism to sue when someone shares highly personal information without consent. The ACLU recommends strengthening Ohio's privacy laws to combat such intrusions of privacy and for the laws to provide a remedy, not to render sexting criminal.

7

Sexting and Charging Juveniles—Balancing the Law and Bad Choices

Mathias H. Heck Jr.

Mathias H. Heck Jr. is prosecuting attorney for Montgomery County, Ohio, and former president of the National District Attorneys Association.

In many cases of teen sexting, juveniles are unaware of proper sexual conduct and that electronically sharing sexually explicit photos of themselves or others may result in felony convictions of child pornography. Therefore, the Montgomery County Juvenile Court in Ohio screens cases to determine if diversion from traditional court proceedings is suitable based on the following factors: whether the juvenile has committed any prior sexual offenses, whether the photos were secured forcibly or under the influence of illicit substances, whether the juvenile has previously participated in a diversion program, or whether the victim or law enforcement strongly opposes diverting the juvenile from the court system. For eligible teens, charging them as sex offenders is unduly harsh, and education and parental involvement is more appropriate.

Katelyn was 15 years old and in love with her 16-year-old boyfriend, Dillon. So, when he asked her to take a naked picture of herself with her cell phone and send it to him, she did. She thought this would be something just the two of them could share and that doing so would show him how much she loved him. But when Dillon broke up with her three weeks later, she started noticing kids at her school giggling behind her back. She soon realized why this was happening when her two best friends came to her and showed her their cell phones, which contained the picture she had sent to Dillon. Her friends told her that the picture had been forwarded to them from their boyfriends and that almost everyone in school had seen the photo or now had it on their phone. For months after that, Katelyn was teased and ridiculed by the other students. She was called printable names like slut, whore, and easy, as well as other names not as printable. Katelyn was devastated. Her grades dropped and she no longer wanted to go to school or socialize with other kids like she used to. Her parents were baffled.

Juveniles engaging in this conduct are completely unaware that what they are doing is illegal, and in many states they could potentially face registration requirements as a sexual offender for committing these acts.

Fourteen-year-old Heather was dating John, her 16-year-old boyfriend. She asked him to take a picture, with her cell phone, of her performing oral sex on him. Heather sent a copy of the picture only to John and he was discrete enough not to share that picture with anyone else, but he did not delete it from his cell phone. John took the cell phone to school and was caught text messaging during class in violation of school policy. The cell phone was confiscated and school personnel believed it to be necessary to look through the phone and found the picture. School authorities decided to report the matter to the police and to contact John's parents. His parents wanted the police to also investigate whether charges should be filed against Heather as the picture was taken at her request with her cell phone.

Such fact patterns have become very common scenarios over the last year, and the practice seems to have no geographic boundaries. Reports from police and educators are so common that this activity has been given its own name— sexting. Sexting is the term given to the act of juveniles sharing sexually explicit or nude cell phone photos of themselves or others. Criminal charges have been filed against teens for sexting in Pennsylvania, Ohio, Michigan, Alabama, Wisconsin, Florida, New York, New Jersey, Connecticut, Texas, Utah and other states.

This relatively new practice among our teen population is a widespread problem—one recent study reports that one in five teens say they have sent or posted online nude photos of themselves.[1] Twenty-two percent of teen girls report doing this, of which half were aged 13–16. In the same report, 31 percent report having received a nude or semi-nude photo from someone else. Approximately two-thirds of these photos are to or from a boyfriend or girlfriend. Shockingly, 15 percent of teens say they have sent nude or semi-nude photos of themselves to someone they only knew online.

The problem that many prosecutors are encountering with these types of cases is that the juveniles engaging in this conduct are completely unaware that what they are doing is illegal, and in many states they could potentially face registration requirements as a sexual offender for committing these acts. In all of the states listed above, prosecutors have charged those sending the photos and those receiving the photos with child pornography offenses.

Under Ohio law, which makes no distinction concerning the age of the "offender" or circumstance, sending such erotic photos of underage minors is typically a felony crime: Pandering Obscenity Involving a Minor, Pandering Sexually Oriented

1. Sex and Tech, Results from a Survey of Teens and Young Adults, The National Campaign to Prevent Teen and Unplanned Pregnancy, October 2008.

Matter Involving a Minor or Illegal Use of a Minor in Nudity-Oriented Material or Performance.

A conviction under one of these felony statutes, which range from a fifth degree felony up to a second degree felony, depending on the circumstances, could also include designation as a Tier I or Tier II sex offender requiring registration for 10 or 20 years.

A unique circumstance that arises in these types of cases is the involvement of the "victim." While in many situations, the person depicted in a state of nudity, the "victim," only intended for the picture to be viewed by a boyfriend or girlfriend, the fact that the picture was transmitted by him or her makes it a crime for which they can also be charged. The victim's charge would be no different than and carry the same penalties as the charge for the person or persons who then forwarded the picture on to their friends.

Recognizing the unique characteristics and possible long term affects that could result from the prosecution of cases similar to those outlined at the beginning of this article, I felt it was important to organize and implement a diversion program for teens accused of sexting.

Charging a juvenile with a felony and labeling them a sexual offender when their actions were clearly a result of poor judgment and ignorance of the law seems harsh for first-time offenders.

The act of sexting appears to be, in at least some cases, a result of our teens not understanding appropriate sexual boundaries and not thinking of the consequences of their actions. That is why on March 4, 2009, the Montgomery County Juvenile Court and I, announced the implementation of the Prosecutor's Juvenile Diversion Program. Under this program, juveniles in Montgomery County, Ohio, who are charged with sexting will be screened by a diversion officer of the Montgomery County Prosecutor's Office to determine if diversion from traditional juvenile court proceedings is appropriate. Some of the factors that will be considered when making that determination are:

- whether the juvenile has any prior sexual offenses,

- whether any type of force or illicit substances were used to secure the photos,

- whether the juvenile has been involved in this particular diversionary program previously, or

- if there is strong opposition by the victim or law enforcement to the juvenile being involved in a diversionary program.

If any of the previous factors are present, it is likely that the juvenile will not be eligible for diversion and will be referred for official action. The purpose behind developing this diversion program is to address first time offenders who engage in this behavior, but are unlikely to re-offend after being educated on the legal ramifications and the possible long term affects on the victim.

The core of the Montgomery County Prosecutor's Juvenile Diversion Program focuses on education but also contains a supervision piece and a community service requirement. If accepted into the diversion program, the juvenile will be under supervision for a minimum of six months, agree to relinquish their cell phone for a period of time, perform community service and attend at least four hours of appropriate and specific education. The educational component will focus on the legal ramifications, the effects on the victim, establishing age appropriate sexual boundaries, and responsible use of the Internet, cell phones and other communication devices. If the program is successfully completed, the charges pending against the juvenile will not be filed or will be dismissed. If it is determined that the juvenile does not meet the criteria to be considered for the diversion program or the juvenile refuses to participate and cooperate, then charges will be filed with the juvenile court.

Certainly, we all want to keep our teens safe from sexual predators and we will not tolerate child pornography being disseminated in our community. However, in some cases, charging a juvenile with a felony and labeling them a sexual offender when their actions were clearly a result of poor judgment and ignorance of the law seems harsh for first-time offenders. It is my belief that this type of activity must be addressed and stopped, and in many cases is best addressed by education and parental involvement.

8

School Officials Must Act to Prevent Sexting and Its Consequences

Morgan J. Aldridge, Susan C. Davies, and Kelli Jo Arndt

At the time of press, Morgan J. Aldridge was a psychology gradu-ate student at the University of Dayton. Susan C. Davies is an assistant professor and coordinator of the school psychology pro-gram at the University of Dayton. Kelli Jo Arndt is an assistant professor and school counseling clinical coordinator at the Uni-versity of Dayton.

School administrators and faculty must be prepared to prevent, plan for, and intervene in the crisis of sexting among students. Prevention efforts should address the risk factors that lead to sexting and offer education programs for both students and teachers. Policy and planning should include an assessment of school resources to combat sexting, of current laws applied to such cases, and of unreported bullying. Research indicates that suspension or expulsion of students involved may be counterpro-ductive. To intervene in incidents of sexting, school administra-tors should determine if contacting law enforcement is appropri-ate, ensure that counselors and other professionals are trained to support students at risk of or affected by sexting, and encourage teachers to look out for distressed students or sexting incidents.

Morgan J. Aldridge, Susan C. Davies, and Kelli Jo Arndt, "Is Your School Prepared for a Sexting Crisis?" *Principal Leadership*, May 2013, pp. 12–16. Copyright © 2013 National Association of Secondary School Principals. All rights reserved. Reprinted with permis-sion.

Preventive education. Educating students and staff members about the risks of sexting is one of the most important factors in preventing and changing the behavior. For instance, 66% of adolescent girls and 60% of adolescent boys report participating in sexting because they think it is "fun or flirtatious." Being accustomed to forwarding anything interesting, students may not think before sending an inappropriate picture to dozens of friends and acquaintances. Helping students understand the social, emotional, and psychological harm sexting can cause, as well as its legal risks, can deter students.

An education-based sexting prevention program in Texas (Before You Text, http://beforeyoutext.com), offers students the opportunity to learn about the consequences of sexting through a series of modules and quizzes. Another interactive resource, Project PRO (Privacy and Reputation Online) educates teens and parents about the potential consequences of online behavior (www.ikeepsafe.org/educators/more/project -pro/3). Sexting also can be incorporated into existing curricula that includes information about appropriate online behavior, bullying, and peer pressure.

Parents and staff members are important to prevention and intervention efforts. School-based mental health professionals can help develop appropriate training for and communications to parents to encourage them to talk to their children and monitor their activities closely.

Policy and Planning

Sexting incidents often require a crisis intervention, so having policies and a plan in place is essential. All elements of the plan should be clearly stated and defined in the school's code of conduct and the crisis team should be prepared to respond to the specific issues involved in sexting. The school crisis team should implement a needs assessment to determine the resources needed to combat sexting, such as curricular materials, training programs, personnel, and school-community partnerships. The needs assessment should also include a survey of students, parents, and staff members to establish the prevalence of sexting in the school district. Policies should be disseminated to students, parents, and staff members so that everyone is aware of the consequences.

It is important that administrators develop sexting-specific policies and ensure that students, parents, and staff members are aware of them.

Current laws. The laws applied in sexting cases are evolving, but currently most are related to child pornography and were not written for sexting situations. Laws differ from state to state, but in many states, students involved in sexting can be charged with felonies, including the production and distribution of child pornography. This charge can lead to mandatory registration as a sex offender. . . .

Because sexting is a crime in most states, school officials are typically required to report sexting incidents to the police. A school resource officer can investigate if a sexting situation is suspected. Police can then obtain search warrants and confiscate phones and computers.

Current school practices. Sexting is considered a form of bullying in many districts and is often governed by general bullying policies. Because sexting can be misconstrued by adolescents as consensual by the original sender of the text or image, however, it is important that administrators develop sexting-specific policies and ensure that students, parents, and staff members are aware of them. As with all behavior policies, simply sending copies of the student handbook home or making the student code of conduct available on the school's website is not enough. Best practice involves verbally communicating sexting policies to all parties, including students, parents, and staff members. Ideally, this verbal communication takes place during orientation, back-to-school activities, and teacher-parent conferences.

Districts have reported using suspension and expulsion as consequences to sexting, but research suggests that disciplinary removal is an ineffective consequence that is associated with several unintended consequences. A more effective remedial consequence might be for all the students involved to receive an in-school suspension during which they learn about the long-term consequences of sexting and receive psychological interventions to help them cope with their actions and prevent similar behaviors from occurring in the future.

> *Suspensions and expulsions [for sexting] may not be in the best interest of the students, especially if they are going to be unsupervised at home.*

Districts should share their sexting policies with local law enforcement agencies so that they understand what kind of role they will be expected to play when sexting incidents occur. In addition, like the underreporting of bullying incidents, principals have indicated that the biggest challenge they encounter is that many incidents go unreported (personal communications). Therefore, school policies should encourage students to come forward while ensuring them that their anonymity will be protected.

Intervention

When a staff member learns about a sexting incident, he or she should report it to an administrator, who will alert the sexting crisis intervention team. If any member of the team (or another staff member) is shown the suspected picture, the phone should be confiscated and law enforcement should be notified. The principal can delegate the following tasks in the crisis plan to crisis team members according to their professional roles.

School administrators. The school administrator determines when it is appropriate to contact law enforcement agencies and the parents of the students who were involved. The administrator is responsible for implementing school-based consequences for both sexting and any subsequent bullying, keeping in mind the emotional effects for both the victim and perpetrators. Suspensions and expulsions may not be in the best interest of the students, especially if they are going to be unsupervised at home, but administrators should also consider that students may face bullying if they remain in school. An alternative is for students to come to school and continue to receive academic instruction and other needed interventions until a decision is made regarding the legality of their actions.

School-based mental health professionals. In addition to their role in prevention and policy development, school psychologists, counselors, and social workers are trained in crisis prevention and intervention, problem solving, and positive behavior supports and interventions. They can counsel students who are at risk for or who have already been affected by sexting and work with families to help minimize the emotional consequences of the incident and prevent the behavior in the future. They also can make appropriate referrals to community-based providers and help coordinate recommended supports provided in school.

Teachers. All teachers should understand the signs of students who may be in distress because of sexting (or bullying), be available to reach out and listen if the student will talk to them, and know the proper referral process. In addition, teachers should be on the lookout for discussions about sexting because an incident will often create a buzz among students. Members of the crisis team or teachers with strong relationships with students can be assigned to spend time in common areas to learn what students are doing and saying. If teachers suspect a sexting incident, they should report what was said and the names of students who were discussing the incident to the appropriate administrator.

Law enforcement agencies. Once administrators have notified law enforcement agencies, as required by law, police officers will conduct a thorough investigation. They may take phones that have been confiscated by school staff members containing the sexting pictures or computers that have been involved in the incident. Law enforcement agencies play a vital role in planning for and responding to sexting crises, and principals should ensure that they are involved in both the prevention of and response to sexting crises.

9

Restricting Sexting May Infringe Free Speech in Schools

Joseph Oluwole and Preston C. Green III

Joseph Oluwole is a professor of education law at Montclair State University in New Jersey. Preston C. Green III is the Harry Lawrence Batschelet II Chair Professor of Educational Administration and professor of education and law at Penn State University. Oluwole and Green are coauthors of Sext Ed: Obscenity Versus Free Speech in Our Schools, *from which the following viewpoint is taken.*

Sexting among teens is controversial in nature, but that alone does not place it under the regulation of schools. In Tinker v. Des Moines Independent Community School District *(1969), the US Supreme Court ruled that school officials must demonstrate actual material and substantial disruption to regulate student speech. Under the* Tinker *standard, sexting—a form of noncommercial, consensual student-to-student speech—cannot be selectively restricted. Furthermore, the Court stated that school officials cannot suppress noncommercial, consensual student-to-student speech expressing sentiments and feelings; students, therefore, do not require approval to use sexting to express themselves. Finally, in* Tinker, *the Court declared that students do not surrender their constitutional right to free speech while on campus, including personal intercommunication such as sexting.*

Joseph Oluwole and Preston C. Green III, *Sext Ed: Obscenity Versus Free Speech in Our Schools.* Santa Barbara, CA: Praeger, 2013, pp. 75–78. Copyright © 2013 ABC-CLIO. All rights reserved. Reprinted with permission.

In any discussions about regulating student speech, we must not lose sight of an important principle—the fact that schools "are educating the young for citizenship is reason for scrupulous protection of Constitutional freedoms of the individual, if we are not to strangle the free mind at its source and teach youth to discount important principles of our government as mere platitudes." The *Tinker* court warned schools that "*more* than a mere desire to avoid the discomfort and unpleasantness that always accompany an unpopular viewpoint" is required in order to prohibit student speech. What is the "more than" that the Constitution requires? According to the Court, the Constitution requires that to regulate speech, schools must show a reasonable forecast of or actual material and substantial disruption of the school's work or infringement of other students' rights; this is the *Tinker* test. The Court found no evidence of a reasonable forecast of or actual "material and substantial" disruption of the school's work or infringement in the *Tinker* case. The students were merely engaged in "silent, passive expression of opinion, unaccompanied by any disorder or disturbance on the part of petitioners."

A school's "urgent wish to avoid the controversy which might result from the expression" is an insufficient ground under the Constitution for regulating student speech. The Court observed that the school officials in *Tinker* had decided to regulate the student speech because the Vietnam War was a "subject of a major controversy." At the time of the school's regulation of the speech, "debate over the Viet Nam war had become vehement in many localities." Additionally, "a protest march against the war had been recently held in Washington, D.C. A wave of draft card burning incidents protesting the war had swept the country. At that time two highly publicized draft card burning cases were pending in this Court. Both individuals supporting the war and those opposing it were quite vocal in expressing their views."

Despite the hot-button nature of the war at the time, the Court ruled that controversialism without material and substantial disruption or infringement of the rights of other students is insufficient grounds to regulate student speech.

When we dehumanize students by failing to acknowledge their individuality and instead seek conformity, we undermine the very premise of the right to free expression.

Today, sexting, while not akin to war, is the "subject of a major controversy." If we follow *Tinker*'s rationale, we know that the controversial nature of sexting alone is not a basis for school regulation of student speech. In essence, based on *Tinker*'s rationale, in order to regulate noncommercial, consensual student-to-student sexting, schools should have to show that such sexting presents a reasonable forecast of or actual material and substantial disruption of the school's work or infringement of other students' rights.

Schools must be wary of selective regulation of student speech. In *Tinker*, the Court chided school officials for selectively regulating the armbands while allowing other "symbols of political or controversial significance": "The record shows that students in some of the schools wore buttons relating to national political campaigns, and some even wore the Iron Cross, traditionally a symbol of Nazism. The order prohibiting the wearing of armbands did not extend to these. Instead, a particular symbol—black armbands worn to exhibit opposition to this Nation's involvement in Vietnam—was singled out for prohibition." This would suggest that if schools selectively regulate noncommercial, consensual student-to-student sexting while allowing other forms of texting, they could lose a court challenge if they fail to satisfy the *Tinker* test. As the Supreme Court indicated in *Tinker*, "Clearly, the prohibition of expression of one particular opinion, at least without evidence that it is necessary to avoid material and substantial interference with schoolwork or discipline, is not constitutionally permissible."

Given the prevailing highly paternalistic attitudes toward students up until *Tinker* was decided, it should not be surprising that the Court went out of its way to explicitly acknowledge that the U.S. Constitution actually regards students as persons: "Students *in* school as well as *out of* school are 'persons' under our Constitution." They are not only persons in and out of school; they actually have "fundamental rights which the State must respect." What a shock that must have been to those who considered students as property and consequently subject to the absolute control of the school. In essence, the Court acknowledged that students have recognized minds of their own. When we dehumanize students by failing to acknowledge their individuality and instead seek conformity, we undermine the very premise of the right to free expression.

Students should not have to seek official approval to engage in noncommercial, consensual student-to-student sexting—a medium for expressing sentiments and feelings.

The Court emphasized that students are not robots to be programmed with the government's choice of message. The Court pointed out that "in our system, state-operated schools may not be enclaves of totalitarianism. School officials do not possess absolute authority over their students. . . . In our system, students may not be regarded as closed-circuit recipients of only that which the State chooses to communicate. They may not be confined to the expression of those *sentiments* that are officially approved."

Sexts express sentiments and feelings; and as the Court stated, "school officials cannot suppress expressions of *feelings* with which they do not wish to contend." Furthermore, it does "violence to both letter and spirit of the Constitution," and we as a people reject "the principle that a State might so conduct its schools as to foster a homogeneous people."

Students should not have to seek official approval to engage in noncommercial, consensual student-to-student sexting—a medium for expressing sentiments and feelings. It is true that not all students sext. Nevertheless, we must protect those who do; after all, we are not a "homogeneous people." Given that schools have a role in helping students define their identities and the fact that speech, including sexting, is part of the process of self-expression and self-identity, schools should not deprive students of this right; nor should punishment attend noncommercial, consensual student-to-student sexting unless there is material and substantial disruption to the school's work or infringement of rights of others. Since it is of the consensual sort, the sexting we refer to herein would not infringe on the rights of others.

Besides, "the vigilant protection of constitutional freedoms is nowhere more vital than in the community of American schools." Before clamping down on noncommercial, consensual student-to-student sexting, let us ask ourselves: should the school not be "peculiarly the marketplace of ideas"? After all, our future as well as the full development of "We the People" (individually and corporately) is dependent on whether we can train our children that effective and democratic learning comes "through wide exposure to that robust exchange of ideas which discovers truth out of a multitude of tongues, [rather] than through any kind of authoritative selection."

The *Tinker* court poignantly declared that "it can hardly be argued that either students or teachers shed their constitutional rights to freedom of speech or expression at the schoolhouse gate." The Court underscored the fact that the principles [of education] . . . are not limited to "supervised and ordained discussion which takes place in the classroom." After all, as the Court eloquently pointed out, "The principal use to which the schools are dedicated is to accommodate students during prescribed hours for the purpose of certain types of activities. Among those activities is *personal intercommunication* among the students." It is undeniable that noncommercial, consensual student-to-student sexting *is* "personal intercommunication among the students" involved. As the Court observed, "personal intercommunication among the students" constitutes "not only an inevitable part of the process of attending school; it is also an important part of the educational process." If we are to uphold the integrity of *Tinker*, we need to be cognizant of the fact that "a student's rights, therefore, do not embrace merely the classroom hours. When he is in the *cafeteria, or on the playing field, or on the campus during the authorized hours,* he may express his opinions, even on *controversial* subjects, . . . if he does so without materially and substantially interfer[ing] with the requirements of appropriate discipline in the operation of the school and without colliding with the rights of others."

Is there any other reason in *Tinker* to extend First Amendment protection to noncommercial, consensual student-to-student sexting? Certainly! First Amendment protection should be extended because "under our Constitution, free speech is not a right that is given only to be so circumscribed that it exists in principle but not in fact. Freedom of expression would not truly exist if the right could be exercised only in an area that a benevolent government has provided as a safe haven for crackpots." Moreover, as the Court stated, "The Constitution says that Congress (and the States) may not abridge the right to free speech. This provision means what it says. . . . We do not confine the permissible exercise of First Amendment rights to a telephone booth or the four corners of a pamphlet, or to supervised and ordained discussion in a school classroom."

10

Sexting Among Older Adults Is Increasing

Jessica Leshnoff

Jessica Leshnoff is a contributing writer for Baltimore Magazine *and AARP.org.*

Adults fifty years old and older are turning to sexting as a fun, easy, and mostly harmless way to spice up their relationships and dating. Some adults sext to feel younger and more lively, while others use it to overcome inhibitions. The convenience of sexting also helps couples stay connected if they have busy schedules or live apart. Nonetheless, sexting has pitfalls for adults, too. Some may send photos to the wrong person or misrepresent their physical appearance and age to others, and not all adults want to receive sexually explicit photos or engage in the activity while first dating.

The injudicious use of a cellphone by former New York Rep. Anthony Weiner has turned the spotlight on sexting—a practice typically associated with teenagers. But the reality is that more and more of the 50-plus set, both single and married, routinely use text messaging to send tantalizing pictures and provocative words to their partner, according to relationship experts.

Most of them are not sexting in the highly public—and, as he acknowledged, "inappropriate"—way that Weiner has admitted to doing. Rather, they are using it as a fun, easy and usually harmless way to spice up their sex.

Relationship coach Suzanne Blake has seen and heard it all when it comes to sexting, including a wife who enjoys sexting her husband while he's traveling on business, telling (and showing) him what he's missing at home. While this may surprise some, Blake's not surprised at all.

"It's a misnomer that the biological changes of aging have to lead to a decrease in sexuality and sexual experience," she says.

Whether they're single and casually dating, married, or in long-term relationships, "Boomers want sexual activity," Blake explains. "They want to flirt. It makes them feel lively and young."

Text Away Your Inhibitions

Jill, 50, certainly feels fresh and vital when she sexts. "It makes you a little more brave," she says. "It takes the fear away, your inhibitions. I might be a little more bold in a text message than I would be over the phone or in person."

Sexting also makes the South Carolina nurse, who's been divorced for 15 years and enjoys casual dating, feel as if she had a "naughty secret."

Sexual health expert Genie James ... recommends sexting to couples who travel a lot, live apart in different cities or have trouble connecting throughout the day.

"If you're sitting in a restaurant waiting for your food, you can just talk dirty to someone, and no one knows what you're doing," Jill says, in a slow Southern drawl. "I would rather talk on the phone. But I'm also comfortable with hiding behind texting if I want to say something dirty."

"That's exactly the appeal of sexting," according to New York psychotherapist and advice columnist Dr. Jonathan Alpert.

"Because there's no anticipation of a direct verbal response, there's less at stake than if the conversation were being held the old-fashioned method: face-to-face," he says. "Where there's less risk of being critiqued or judged, there's opportunity for greater sexual expression."

Stay Connected

"It also fits nicely into longtime couples' busy schedules to keep things spicy," says relationship and sexual health expert Genie James, who recommends sexting to couples who travel a lot, live apart in different cities or have trouble connecting throughout the day. "It's cheap," she says. "It's quick. It's right there. And nobody can hear you."

James continues, "It's about setting the stage for sex and keeping passion alive. A cellphone's in your hands every day. You're already doing it."

But beware, the experts warn. Sexting has its dangers, too. For one thing, it can be easy to send a text to a wrong number, and that can be embarrassing—or worse.

When it comes to dating, false advertising is often a big issue, says relationship expert Dr. Gilda Carle. It's something online daters may be all too familiar with when their date shows up looking about 30 years older than his profile photo.

Don't Get Carried Away with Sexting

"They're overselling and over-promising," she says of big-talking sexters. "I think too much, too soon in relationships is not such a great thing. I suggest to people that you grow the relationship outside the bedroom so that when you come into the bedroom, it's your playpen." Then there's the comfort factor. Not everyone likes having a sexually charged text or photo pop up on her phone as much as she thought she would.

Richard, 66, received an X-rated photo on his cellphone from a potential online date recently and surprised himself by being less than thrilled.

"It was a little bit embarrassing," the Iowa resident says sheepishly. "Well, it was very embarrassing."

The fact that he was with a group of colleagues after hours at a restaurant didn't help matters, either.

Sexting might be an interesting experiment, he says with a sigh, but after his experience, "It was like the fun kind of went out of it."

11

Sexting Is Rooted in Primal Urges

Ogi Ogas

Ogi Ogas is a cognitive neuroscientist and coauthor of A Billion Wicked Thoughts: What the Internet Tells Us About Sexual Relationships.

The urge to sext originates from evolutionary behaviors. However, there are key gender differences to why people flaunt their bodies in self-portraits. Female exhibitionism is driven by the desire to be sexually attractive; women find it arousing to be the center of erotic attention. Studies reveal that the majority of women fantasize about being in such scenarios. On the other hand, men show their genitals to indicate their sexual interest; the practice is evident among primates and cultures around the world. While such displays are often deemed offensive, male exhibitionism is generally viewed as harmless by psychologists—most men do not seek contact after flashing their genitalia to strangers.

Over the past two years [2010 to 2012], more photographs of bare-naked celebrity anatomy have been leaked to the public eye than over the previous two centuries: Scarlett Johansson snapping a blurry self-portrait while sprawled on her bed, Vanessa Hudgens posing for a cellphone in a bracelet and a smile, Congressman [Anthony] Weiner touting a Blackberry and a mirror in the House Members Gym, Jessica Alba, Christina Aguilera, Miley Cyrus, Ron Artest, Charlize Theron, Chris Brown, Bret Favre, Rihanna, Pete Wentz, Ke$ha, and dozens more.

This flood of celebrity skin has prompted folks to wonder, "Why are so many famous people exhibitionists?" The source of all this *au naturel* flaunting lies not in the culture of fame, but in the design of our sexual brains. In fact, research has unveiled two distinct explanations: Female exhibitionism appears to be primarily cortical, while male exhibitionism is mainly subcortical.

The Desire to Be Sexually Irresistible

"The desire of the man is for the woman," Madame de Stael [an eighteenth-century French writer] famously penned. "The desire of the woman is for the desire of the man." Being the center of sexual attention is a fundamental female turn-on dramatized in women's fantasies, female-authored erotica, and in the cross-cultural gush of sultry self-portraits.

Studies have found that more than half of women's sexual fantasies reflect the desire to be sexually irresistible. In one academic survey, 47 percent of women reported the fantasy of seeing themselves as a striptease dancer, harem girl, or other performer. Fifty percent fantasized about delighting many men.

Whereas male exhibitionism is considered a psychiatric disorder and sometimes a crime, female exhibitionism is rarely considered a social problem.

"Being desired is very arousing to women," observes clinical psychologist Marta Meana, president of the Society for Sex Therapy and Research. "An increasing body of data is indicating that the way women feel about themselves may be very important to their experience of sexual desire and subjective arousal, possibly even outweighing the impact of their partners' view of them."

The source of all this *au naturel* flaunting lies not in the culture of fame, but in the design of our sexual brains.

The desire to be desired drives young women's willingness to enter wet T-shirt contests and flash what their mama gave them at Mardi Gras. Whereas male exhibitionism is considered a psychiatric disorder and sometimes a crime, female exhibitionism is rarely considered a social problem. Just the opposite: It's exploited commercially. Multi-millionaire Joe Francis built his Girls Gone Wild empire by taping college girls stripping down for his no-budget camera crew. How does he persuade young women to disrobe? He offers them a T-Shirt and a chance to be ogled by millions of men.

"Look I'm human, & just like every girl in this world, I admire my body so i take pics," wrote singer Teyana Taylor after her graphic self-portraits were leaked. International data supports Taylor's contention that the female exhibitionist urge is universal. In Brazil, Japan, Ghana, and the USA, well-trafficked websites offer galleries of tens of thousands of racy amateur self-portraits surreptitiously downloaded from women's private MySpace or Facebook accounts or maliciously provided by ex-boyfriends. It's not just celebrities who share intimate imagery.

A Display of Sexual Interest

Though men are so eager to gaze upon women's candid photos they're willing to risk jail time by hacking cellphones, pictures of men's private parts usually come to public attention when a recipient is offended; German Olympian Ariane Friedrich, for example, outed a man on Facebook for sending her a photograph of his manhood. These pickle shots tend to elicit protests and consternation. Men do not question why Scarlett Johansson or Jessica Alba might want to sext bare skin to a guy. But women everywhere ask, "What are men thinking when they send us photos of their junk?" The answer is that men may not be thinking at all; they may be compelled by an unconscious, evolutionary urge inherited from our primate ancestors.

Male monkeys and apes routinely display their penises to females to indicate sexual interest. Primatologist Frans de Waal writes in *Peacemaking Among Primates*:

> Since bonobos can sheath their penis, nothing is visible most of the time. When the organ does appear, however, it is not only impressive in size, but its bright pink color makes it stand out against the dark fur. Males invite others by presenting with legs wide apart and back arched, often flicking the penis up and down—a powerful signal.

Though hordes of men pay to peruse amateur photography depicting the anatomy of ladies, not a single website collects cash from ladies interested in surveying amateur photography of phalluses.

Men do not share women's desire to be desired. Instead, they emulate their bonobo brethren: The internet is saturated with penis self-portraits from every nation on Earth. At any given moment, one in four cameras on the webcam network ChatRoulette are aimed at a penis. On the adult networking site Fantasti.cc, 36 percent of men use an image of a penis as their avatar; only 5 percent of women use a vagina. On Reddit's heterosexual Gone Wild forum in 2010, where users were free to post uncensored pictures of themselves, 35 percent of images self-posted by men consisted of penises.

Anyone who has seen a koteka, the elaborate two-foot-long penis cap worn by men in Papua New Guinea, can easily believe that men have inherited our hominid cousins' exhibitionist urge regarding the penis. In fact, male exhibitionism has long been understood by clinical psychologists as a nondangerous compulsion: Men who flash their organ to strangers rarely seek contact afterward, instead describing a powerful sense of relief from the display alone. Of course, the yawn is also a powerful biological compulsion, but as we learned in grade school it's always preferable to cover your mouth.

Dichotomous Evolutionary Pressures

Though hordes of men pay to peruse amateur photography depicting the anatomy of ladies, not a single website collects cash from ladies interested in surveying amateur photography of phalluses. It is this marked gender difference in interest that reveals the dichotomous evolutionary pressures shaping male and female exhibitionism: Women feel the conscious desire to catch the universally attentive male eye, but since women's erotic attention is rarely ensnared by a penis, the male exhibitionist urge is comparatively vestigial.

There are profitable penis sites, however. They boast an engaged clientele who view male sexting as neither troubling nor distasteful and reveal the universality of male sexual circuitry. Who appreciates leaked shots of *The Game*'s well-endowed Hosea Chanchez with the same enthusiasm heterosexual guys show for leaked shots of *Mad Men*'s well-endowed Christina Hendricks? Gay men.

12

Is Sexting Someone Else "Cheating"?

Louisa Peacock

Louisa Peacock is deputy women's editor of The Telegraph, *a British newspaper.*

As digital communication transforms the notions of romance and relationships, whether the act of sexting behind a partner's back is cheating is a complicated issue. Some psychologists contend that sexting is different than having a physical affair, and its emotional motivations—being provocative or an exhibitionist—does not necessarily involve a genuine romantic interest. However, others maintain that the shame and humiliation of sexting can impact a relationship. Also, dealing with the partner's lies, knowing of shared intimacies, and confusion can be as harmful as physical cheating. In the end, sexting is not all fantasy—it is a form of engagement with someone else.

If you haven't already seen this video, watch it. There is something rather eerie about [politician] Anthony Weiner's wife, Huma Abedin, standing dutifully beside him as he reads out an apologetic but vaguely-worded statement about him sexting another woman under the pseudonym 'Carlos Danger.'

She stands gracefully at his side throughout. At one point she smiles at someone in the audience. At another point she nods at his words. Next, she's speaking herself, about how she's "forgiven" him and "moving forward" from the scandal. Wow. Her on-screen performance is remarkable.

Like her close confidante Mrs [Hillary] Clinton, the former first lady and secretary of state, whose husband was also involved in a sex scandal, Miss Abedin has chosen to stand by her man.

Again: wow. I don't know if I could ever be that forgiving if I found out my husband had been sexting someone else. Let alone declare that I've forgiven him in public. Think about it: would you? Sexting is not physical sex. Neither is it traditional "cheating" as we all know it. Then again, it doesn't just live in the land of pure fantasy, either. It requires the physical act of sending a message and engaging with another person—behind your partner's back.

Whether or not "sexting" is cheating is a really tricky one to call. Of course, it depends on so many things—the relationship you're in, how long you've been together, how open your relationship is, how often your partner was "sexting" behind your back, and to whom, and so on. But if it did happen to you, how on earth would you deal with it? As online, social media and smartphone communication blurs the boundaries about what a romantic relationship is, it's not obvious where "sexting" fits in the modern age.

It could be that the "sexter" enjoys being provocative, or likes to be an exhibitionist, for example; it's not necessarily about infidelity or lusting after someone else.

Let's think about this. On a scale where having a full-blown affair is at one end, and your partner never having so much as looked at another person sexually before is at the other, where would you put sexting? In a scenario where your man was sending sexually graphic images of himself to another woman, but had to date had no physical contact with her, where would you put that? I instinctively hover on the "cheating" side of the fence—it's an emotional cheat, isn't it?—before hesitating and jumping back over to the "harmless" side: there's no physical affair taking place.

Having said that, in some ways, an "emotional"-only cheat is harder to stomach than a purely physical act. A friend of mine once found out her husband was cheating on her with another woman: when he said he "loved" the other woman, that was more hurtful to her than the thought of them having sex together. I can see where she's coming from.

So Is Sexting "Cheating"?

But sexting *is* different to having a physical affair, psychologists tell me. Dr Teri Apter, a psychologist, writer and senior tutor at the University of Cambridge, says the emotional reasons for sexting are not necessarily the same for carrying out a physical affair. It could be that the "sexter" enjoys being provocative, or likes to be an exhibitionist, for example; it's not necessarily about infidelity or lusting after someone else. They may still love and fancy you, but "sext" someone else purely as a means of escapist fantasy. It's childish and stupid and in hindsight, hurtful to you, but isn't necessarily a sign of infidelity.

The truth is, I wouldn't know how to deal with my partner "sexting" someone else behind my back. Until it happens (and for the record, I hope it never does), I don't know how I'm going to react. And different people will obviously react differently depending on a variety of factors that suggest sexting should be "judged", if that's the right word, on a case-by-case basis.

Dr Apter agrees there is no one-size-fits-all approach to sexting; and that how you deal with your partner sending sexually explicit messages to someone else behind your back is subjective.

But, she says, it's not as clear cut as saying that sexting amounts to cheating. "You can love someone and be committed and faithful in deed but there will be aspects of a fantasy life that comes into play. For example, if you go to a film, or watch a play, and feel a desire for one of the characters but don't act upon it [i.e. it stays in the cinema; in that moment of watching the film], then that doesn't feel like infidelity. It's just a motor idling desire that doesn't have any impact on other people."

People often take issue with their partners sexting not for the sexual, emotional "affair" itself, but for the fact he/she could even take part in such a "shameful", "childlike" act.

With sexting and sending messages, 'sexters' have a persona that develops which happens in the flick of an eye "but doesn't change the emotional gears of real life," she says.

'It's the Humiliation and Shame That's the Bigger Problem'

The minute the 'sexter' gets found out for sexting, however, the matter is out in the open and it switches from being a fantasy-led to a real-life scenario—one that has the power to humiliate and cause feelings of betrayal in their partner.

"You realise that your partner has this almost childlike, macho fantasy and it's demeaning for you. It can become intolerable because of the 'shaming' aspect: you've made a statement publicly that you're together, whether married or in a relationship, and yet his crude sexting has affected that."

Dr Apter explains that people often take issue with their partners sexting not for the sexual, emotional "affair" itself, but for the fact he/she could even take part in such a "shameful", "childlike" act and risk humiliating them in the process.

So she says "there is an element of cheating because it's a relationship in which the fantasy is enacted, but it doesn't have the deed of actual sex. The bigger impact is often on the marriage itself and you learning that your partner is not the person they thought they were".

As Dr Petra Boynton, a social psychologist lecturing in international health care at University College London (and Telegraph Wonder Women's agony aunt), puts it: "The consequences of being lied to, knowing your partner was sharing intimacies with someone else, or trying to convince you it's all in your head/not a problem can be as devastating as if someone's cheated physically."

Laying Down the Ground Rules

Ultimately, it's up to individuals to decide what constitutes fidelity in their relationship. But it would help if you both communicated that in the early stages to avoid upset/disappointment/confusion.

Says Dr Boyton: "If you find yourself sharing flirty or sexual conversations with someone and are pretty sure you'd be upset if you knew your partner did the same or that your partner would be upset if they read your messages then you can be fairly sure you're on your way to cheating or already invested in an emotional affair.

"People can and do recover from such situations, sometimes if caught early they can serve as a reminder of the importance of a primary relationship. Some require counselling and complete transparency and openness from a cheating partner—including clear signs said partner is doing all they can to make amends. Not everyone can move on, particularly if a physical relationship and greater deceptions were also involved."

The different factors involved almost make it impossible to answer the blanket question of whether sexting is cheating, and more to the point, whether you would forgive your partner for doing it behind your back. I'm still hovering from one side of the fence to the other, but if I really had to choose, then deep down I have to sit more on the "cheating" side. Just because something isn't sexually physical doesn't make it pure fantasy: the fact is, sexting is a relationship of sorts, where the sexter engages with someone else behind your back, and that has the power to be just as hurtful as a full-blown affair with another person.

Organizations to Contact

The editors have compiled the following list of organizations concerned with the issues debated in this book. The descriptions are derived from materials provided by the organizations. All have publications or information available for interested readers. The list was compiled on the date of publication of the present volume; names, addresses, phone and fax numbers, and e-mail and Internet addresses may change. Be aware that many organizations take several weeks or longer to respond to inquiries, so allow as much time as possible.

AASA, the School Superintendents Association
1615 Duke St., Alexandria, VA 22314
(703) 528-0700 • fax: (703) 841-1543
e-mail: info@aasa.org
website: www.aasa.org

Founded in 1865, AASA, the School Superintendents Association, is a professional organization of more than thirteen thousand educational leaders in the United States and throughout the world. It works to advance the goals of public education and champion children's causes in their districts. The AASA website offers information on sexting and cyberbullying.

Beatbullying
+44 20 8771-3377 • fax: +44 20 8771-8550
e-mail: info@beatbullying.org
website: www.beatbullying.org

Beatbullying works with children and teenagers across the United Kingdom to provide important opportunities to change their lives and outlook positively. In particular, the organization works with those so deeply affected by bullying that they fear going to school. Beatbullying also seeks to effect change in bullies' behavior, working with them to take responsibility and a sense of ownership over their actions. Videos, news, and resources for youths, families, and professionals are offered on its website.

Childnet International

Studio 14, Brockley Cross Business Centre
96 Endwell Rd., London   SE4 2PD
+44 20 7639-6967 • fax: +44 20 7639-7027
e-mail: info@childnet.com
website: www.childnet.com

Childnet International is dedicated to helping young people constructively use the Internet. The organization gives Internet safety advice and links for children, teenagers, parents, and teachers. Policy papers and annual reviews are available online.

ConnectSafely

www.connectsafely.org

ConnectSafely is a forum for parents, teens, educators, and advocates designed to give teens and parents a voice in the public discussion about youth online safety. The site offers tips for safe social networking as well as other resources.

CTIA—The Wireless Association

1400 Sixteenth St. NW, Suite 600, Washington, DC   20036
(202) 736-3200 • fax: (202) 785-0721
website: www.ctia.org

CTIA—The Wireless Association is an international nonprofit membership organization founded in 1984, representing all sectors of wireless communications—cellular, personal communication services, and enhanced specialized mobile radio. Information on wireless safety is provided on its website.

Cyberbully411

website: www.cyberbully411.org

Cyberbully411 provides resources and opportunities for discussion and sharing for teenagers who want to know more about—or have been victims of—online harassment. The website was created by the nonprofit Internet Solutions for Kids, Inc. and invites teenagers to share their stories or download tips and information on cyberbullying, depression, and other relevant topics.

Federal Trade Commission (FTC)

600 Pennsylvania Ave. NW, Washington, DC   20580

(202) 326-2222

website: www.ftc.gov

The Federal Trade Commission (FTC) deals with issues of everyday economic life. It is the only federal agency with both consumer protection and competition jurisdiction. The FTC strives to enforce laws and regulations and advance consumers' interests by sharing its expertise with federal and state legislatures and US and international government agencies. Articles such as "Understanding Mobile Apps" can be downloaded from its website.

Institute for Responsible Online and Cell-Phone Communication (I.R.O.C.^{2})

PO Box 1131, 200 Walt Whitman Ave.

Mount Laurel, NJ   08054-9998

(877) 295-2005

website: www.iroc2.org

The Institute for Responsible Online and Cell-Phone Communication (I.R.O.C.^{2}) is a nonprofit organization advocating digital responsibility, safety, and awareness. It endorses the development and safe use of all digital devices (e.g., digital cameras, cell phones, computers, Internet, video cameras, web cameras, and so on) and the World Wide Web. The organization's creation is based on the fact that many individuals are not aware of the short- and long-term consequences of their own actions when utilizing digital technologies. Articles on social networking and sexting are available online.

Internet Keep Safe Coalition

4301 N. Fairfax Dr., Suite 190, Arlington, VA 22203
(703) 717-9066 • fax: (703) 852-7100
website: www.iKeepSafe.org

Internet Keep Safe Coalition is nonprofit international alliance of more than one hundred policy leaders, educators, law enforcement members, technology experts, public health experts, and advocates. Through this network of support, the organization tracks global trends and issues surrounding digitally connected products and their effects on children. This research aims to provide resources for parents, educators, and policy makers who seek to teach youths how to use new media devices and platforms in safe and healthy ways.

Internet Solutions for Kids

1820 E. Garry Ave., Suite 105, Santa Ana, CA 92705
(877) 302-6858 • fax: (877) 362-1629
e-mail: info@isolutions4kids.org
website: http://is4k.com

Internet Solutions for Kids is a nonprofit research organization that explores the impact of new technologies on adolescent health. The organization seeks to promote innovative methods that improve the health and safety of young people, engaging in research as well as active youth education and support. The organization created the website Cyberbully 411.org.

WiredSafety

website: www.wiredsafety.org

WiredSafety is an Internet safety and help group. It provides educational material, news, assistance, and awareness on all aspects of cybercrime and abuse, privacy, security, and responsible technology use. It is also the parent group of Teen angels.org, a website run by teens who were trained by the Federal Bureau of Investigation (FBI), and Tweenangels.org, which uses the knowledge and insights of preteens in an effort to promote Internet safety.

Bibliography

Books

Nancy K. Baym   *Personal Connections in the Digital Age*. Malden, MA: Polity, 2010.

Howard Gardner and Katie Davis   *The App Generation: How Today's Youth Navigate Identity, Intimacy, and Imagination in a Digital World*. New Haven, CT: Yale University Press, 2013.

Sameer Hinduja and Justin W. Patchin   *School Climate 2.0: Preventing Cyberbullying and Sexting One Classroom at a Time*. Thousand Oaks, CA: Corwin, 2012.

Janell Burley Hofmann   *iRules: What Every Tech-Healthy Family Needs to Know About Selfies, Sexting, Gaming, and Growing Up*. Emmaus, PA: Rodale Books, 2014.

Tom Jacobs   *Teen Cyberbullying Investigated: Where Do Your Rights End and Consequences Begin?* Minneapolis, MN: Free Spirit Publishing, 2010.

Andrew Keen   *Digital Vertigo: How Today's Online Social Revolution Is Dividing, Diminishing, and Disorienting Us*. New York: St. Martin's Press, 2012.

Robin M. Kowalski, Susan P. Limber, and Patricia W. Agatston   *Cyberbullying: Bullying in the Digital Age*, 2nd ed. Malden, MA: Wiley-Blackwell, 2012.

| Ogi Ogas and Sai Gaddam | *A Billion Wicked Thoughts: What the Internet Tells Us About Sexual Relationships.* New York: Dutton, 2011. |

| Larry D. Rosen | *iDisorder: Understanding Our Obsession with Technology and Overcoming Its Hold on Us.* New York: Palgrave Macmillan, 2012. |

| Robert Weiss and Jennifer P. Schneider | *Closer Together, Further Apart: The Effect of Technology and the Internet on Parenting, Work, and Relationships.* Carefree, AZ: Gentle Path Press, 2014. |

Periodicals and Internet Sources

| Sand Avidar-Walzer | "A Freudian Analysis of Texting," *Salon*, August 1, 2013. www.salon.com. |

| Art Bowker and Michael Sullivan | "Sexting: Risky Actions and Overreactions," *FBI Law Enforcement Bulletin*, July 2010. |

| Nina Burleigh | "Sexting, Shame, and Suicide," *Rolling Stone*, September 17, 2013. |

| Glenda Cooper | "Sexting: A New Teen Cyber-Bullying 'Epidemic,'" *Telegraph*, April 12, 2012. |

| Jamie Lynn Fletcher and Vik Jolly | "'Sexting': Self-Destructive or Simple Rebellion?," *Orange County Register*, March 20, 2009. |

| Jan Hoffman | "A Girl's Nude Photo, and Altered Lives," *New York Times*, March 26, 2011. |

Casey Johnston   "Sexting: It's Not Just for Teens Anymore," *Ars Technica*, February 12, 2014. http://arstechnica.com.

Elizabeth Meyer   "Sexting and Suicide," *Gender and Schooling,*, December 16, 2009. www.psychologytoday.com/blog /gender-and-schooling.

Mitch Mitchell   "A Teacher, Sexting, and the Right to Free Speech," *Fort Worth Star-Telegram*, February 25, 2014.

A. Pawlowski   "Seventh-Graders Sexting? It Might Be More Common Than You Think," *Today*, January 6, 2014. www.today .com/moms.

Leonard Sax   "Blame Parents, Not Kids, for Sexting," *Wall Street Journal*, October 24, 2013.

Jeff R. Temple et al.   "Teen Sexting and Its Association with Sexual Behaviors," *JAMA Pediatrics*, September 2012.

Penelope Trunk   "The Joys of Adult Sexting," Daily Beast, June 6, 2011. www.dailybeast .com.

Index